The

Mark

SHE KEPT

"A Woman's Journey to, Living her

Purpose Courageously"

Ferrin Roy

This book is dedicated to my mother.

Thank you for accepting my birthmark as a part of me, because of your wisdom, I am living my purpose in life.

---.---

"If you celebrate your differentness, the world will too. It believes exactly what you tell it, through words you use to describe yourself, the actions you take to care for yourself, and the choices you make to express yourself. Tell the world you are one-of-a-kind creation who came here to experience wonder and spread joy. Expect to be accommodated."

Victoria Moran

---.---

Table of Contents

Preface

I am not a psychiatrist. I'm a realist, sharing my personal experiences of living with my facial birthmark for 30 years. I was born with a large facial birthmark on my right cheek which I have grown to love and cherish. I refer to it as my beauty mark. The journey to accepting the way I was created, has been one of self-realization.

I hope this book reaches the hands of anyone who struggles with being different. Someone debating plastic surgery because of depression, parents who are raising a child with a facial birthmark or an insecure individual with a face disfigurement or scar. My goal is to encourage you because not only do I understand the struggles you may encounter, but I've lived them as well. I challenge you to, "UNVEIL YOUR FACE!" Raise your head high! You are distinguished and beautiful.

Your face may not be ordinary, but that alone makes you more interesting!

This book will explain in detail how I've evolved with my birthmark and the cycles that took place at every stage of my life. Hopefully, my journey will help you understand that you can overcome your fears and insecurities, and embrace the beautiful life that is ahead of you.

Introduction

Today, people look at me and wonder why I'm so confident, or why I'm not broken or insecure. The truth is, I have been broken and insecure. I've cried, shied away from being noticed, debated surgery and valued others' opinion more than my own. There were days I was embarrassed about my birthmark. Days I wondered why did God choose me to have a birthmark. Days I felt so timid and insecure because so many eyes were staring at me at once. Days when I didn't feel like defending my birthmark. There were many days I wished it would just go away, but this journey has amazingly led me to loving my birthmark, and it's all because of growth! I feel so free now! I often listen to Kirk Franklin's song - *Imagine Me*. Imagine me, being free, of insecurities! I know my purpose, and it's to encourage others to love themselves. Today, I love it when people inquire about my birthmark. My beauty cannot be compared to anyone else because of its uniqueness. I don't desire to look like anyone else nor do I consider my birthmark a flaw. I don't cover my birthmark with makeup, and I no longer wonder what people will say upon meeting me for the first time. Stares no longer bother me because I understand that people are naturally inquisitive. The reality is that "different" isn't always acceptable in society, but it is important to ask yourself, "who am I living for?" Don't spend your entire life trying to change anyone's perception of you. Think about the world we live in; people criticize physical appearances every day! People get Botox injections, nostril surgeries, lip surgeries, etc. just to fit the profile "society" feels is acceptable. This new era is about being "flawless!" Photoshoots are taking place more frequently on social media and honestly, some of them have no meaning. Some trends promote a healthier lifestyle while others only cause people to criticize themselves. Some people spend hours comparing themselves to others. People are so scared to be their authentic selves. Filters were created to cover blemishes and create a "flawless" look. Do you realize that people will find a "flaw" in you no matter what you do? People zoom into pictures to find a loose string on your blouse, or an item missed from the background of your picture.

Let's be realistic; of course, people will criticize your birthmark, stare, and make comments. What matters is how you receive the information. I've met people who had no idea what a birthmark was. I've also encountered individuals who knew what it was and made jokes about it. I've always stood up for myself. I love defending my birthmark because it is mine. I've heard statements such as, "It'll be hard to rob a bank with that!" My response, "Never thought about robbing a bank and actually succeeding but thanks!" or "Oh my, how can she be so confident with that?" My response, "Because I'm comfortable in my skin." I've also heard positive things as well. People have complimented me as being beautiful with it. I hear this comment often. "Beautiful with it." In my mind, I'm beautiful without the extra emphasis. I understand that there are incividuals who really have no idea what a birthmark is. Educating others about birthmarks will not only help them recognize one, but it will also help them understand that birthmarks can be anywhere on the body. For my readers who do not know what a birthmark is, here's a brief explanation.

Birthmarks are present at birth or appear shortly after birth. They appear in various textures, shapes, and sizes. Birthmarks are not contagious or hereditary. Doctors explain that birthmarks are caused by an overgrowth of blood vessels in the skin. Some people believe old folk tales that state they are caused by cravings experienced by the birth mother. My mother said she was craving strawberries at the time and my grandfather couldn't find them anywhere. She believes it's a strawberry. The scientific term for my birthmark is a nevus. Once a year, I visit my dermatologist to make sure the pigmentation hasn't changed, and it's healthy. Some birthmarks cause abnormal growth, bleeding, and cancer. The *Vascular Birthmark Foundation* provides more insight on vascular birthmarks, research studies, and surgical doctors. You can get more information by visiting http://www.birthmark.org

Thankfully, I haven't had any medical issues with my birthmark. It hasn't grown any larger since I was born or changed its pigmentation. Now that you have more insight, it's time to build courage for your unique appearance. Here's my story.

The Mark

My mother was a teenage mom; she had me at the age of 17. I can't help but think that teenage pregnancies were uncommon in 1987 and therefore an embarrassment for the soon-to-be mother and her parents. I can only imagine the awkward stares she received being pregnant along with the comments that were mentioned at school. My mother and I discussed how complicated it was being pregnant as a teenager, working a full-time job and attending high school. She was one of seven siblings in her household along with my grandmother, and when I was born, I became everyone's bundle of joy. Weighing in at 6lbs 11oz and healthy with a large nevus birthmark on my right cheek. No one present at my birth noticed the birthmark but my grandfather. Once it was confirmed as a nevus, the doctors explained to my parents the risk factors pertaining to skin cancer and some situations people with birthmarks tend to experience like teasing, and depression. My mother never saw anyone with a facial birthmark similar to mine, so she was unsure whether to remove it or allow me to make my own decision once I was a little older. I like to envision myself in my mother's shoes. Not only was she a teenage mom dealing with varying reactions from the community, she now has a huge decision to make on something about which she knows absolutely nothing. She began thinking about what my life would be like; would I be ashamed of it or would I blame her? After discussing amongst the family, my parents decided they would allow me to make the decision once I became a little older.

My parents divorced when I was four years old, but my father remained actively present in my life. Years later, my stepfather entered my life as well. My mother never tried to hide my birthmark or comb my hair a particular way to camouflage it. She always told me how beautiful and unique I was. I believed her. She never felt sorry for me, and I could feel the genuineness of her assurance. One memory that will stick with me forever is my mother touching my birthmark and rubbing her face against mine.

"A simple sense of touch felt like a breath of fresh air;
SHE EMBRACED IT!"

Prior to attending school, my mom told me, "Ferrin, this is your birthmark." You may not see other kids with one, but it's for you and you are special. Children may ask you about it, just answer them and smile. If anyone teases you, tell the teacher."

My mother was 21 at the time I began school. She was instilling confidence in me at the age of four, encouraging me to take ownership of my birthmark. I can't recall many experiences during primary grades where I was teased. I was born and raised in Rayne, Louisiana. Yes, I'm a country girl. I love gumbo, crawfish, and boudin! I attended grade school with the same kids until 12th grade. I believe this made my childhood years easier because everyone was used to seeing my birthmark. When I asked my mother if she recalls any teasing experiences I encountered as a child, she said:

"You don't remember, but you were teased by a boy in school. You told me he called you ugly. I asked you what you said to him, and you said, "I'm pretty, and he is mean.""

I was curious, so I asked my mother if she would she have considered homeschooling had the teasing continued, she said,

"No, because you needed to be prepared for the world outside of our home."

*****

From my mother's heart

"When I first saw you, you were lying in the incubator with the birthmark side of your check faced down. I immediately insisted that the nurse turn your cheek so that the birthmark was visible. I told the nurse we had nothing to be ashamed of. During my two-day hospital stay, each time I visited you were lying with the birthmark face up. When visitors arrived, I would also inquire which position you were in. Somehow, I knew with all my heart at 17 years that God made the decision to allow this to happen and I would accept it. So many children were born unhealthy during our time at the hospital. You were healthy, beautiful, and loved.

To all parents struggling with acceptance from others:

I knew it was my job as her mother to teach her to be proud of her looks. I basically taught her how she should be treated. Others would have to accept her appearance; it was not an option to have it removed unless she wanted to.

The power of prayer is one of God's greatest gifts! I prayed for her to be able to stand up to those who stare, make jokes or ask questions at an early age. There were several instances when I was questioned by adults (in doctor's offices, at the grocery store, at school, etc.) as to why I didn't or wouldn't remove it. Several inappropriate comments were also made like, 'What's wrong with her?' 'What happened?' 'Does it hurt?' 'Is it a burn?' 'That's a shame because she is so pretty.', etc.

My usual response was, "She was born this way, and this is how God wants my baby to look!" However, there were also times in which I would stare at the adults staring at her, and the birthmark was no longer a focus.

I also would say, "She was kissed by an angel on her right cheek." I've always encouraged her to love who she is, and if ever she decided to remove her birthmark, it was her choice. I'm so happy Ferrin decided on her own to keep it. I'm so proud that she is my daughter. Who would have known that I, pregnant at 17, would give birth to a confident woman who would inspire so many others to love themselves?

*****

I don't recall my mother making my birthmark the topic of discussion whenever we were invited to birthday parties, events, or play dates. Imagine a child who hears their parents constantly discussing wanting to remove their birthmark, wouldn't that decrease their self-esteem especially if they are experiencing complications outside of the home? I understand some people feel that acknowledging it before someone says something may defuse the attention your child may receive but remember, your thoughts can consume you.

"Our thoughts, if unchecked, can sometimes take us into dark spaces created by our own will."

I was spoiled as a child. My godmother, aunts, uncles, and cousins would take me everywhere. No one was ashamed of me. I have a close relationship with every single one of them. I spoke with my aunts and uncles about this, and they all said I wouldn't be "Ferrin" without it. I was surrounded by love. If I was kissed, it was not a preference to kiss the cheek without the birthmark. It was a part of my face, and everyone cuddled and kissed me just as if it wasn't there.

- -

'You are the only you God made...God made you and broke the mold."

Max Lucado

- -

I encourage all families of children with birthmarks to touch, embrace and kiss your child's birthmark. Allow your child to become familiar with it as well. Stand in front of the mirror and play simple games such as "hands, ears, and eyes." Incorporate the location of the birthmark, while doing so. By incorporating the birthmark, you are helping them come to the realization that it is a part of them. What I remember as a child is dressing up as a princess, playing pretend school with stuffed animals and running around outside with the neighborhood kids. I remember a blue and white swing my mom purchased for me, everyone in the neighborhood thought I was such a cool kid because I was the only one in the neighborhood with one. I can't recall if my friends ever asked about my birthmark. At such a young age, I couldn't recognize stares or fully understand what was going on even if my family was questioned about it. I was free! What I didn't realize was that the older I became, the more this would change. Children only have eyes for certain things at this age such as swings, bikes, candy, cartoons, games, etc. As a parent, however, you will notice stares from older people sometimes you can feel the stares from afar. You are the voice for your child when they are young and may find yourself constantly explaining and defending their unique look.

My parents had to explain to several people what was on my cheek. Some were respectful questions, but others were not. My mom heard this phrase often, "She marked her baby." This phrase is in reference to my mom craving strawberries during her pregnancy. Some parents are constantly defending their child; they get so overwhelmed and consider removal their only option. Can you imagine being a parent and having people stare at your child everywhere you go as if they don't belong in this world? Many parents live these moments frequently as they try to create a normal life for their child.

Children experience teasing at such a young age and are crying out for acceptance. Some children cry every day, wondering why they were chosen to have a birthmark. Most children do not adapt well to change and prefer being around the same people whom they feel comfortable with. Some parents console their children at night because they are depressed about being different. Some parents blame themselves. There are also parents who travel the world in search of the best surgical doctor, to remove the birthmark because medical treatment is necessary. Others feel forced to remove the birthmark because of emotional trauma. Several children experience these emotions today and unfortunately may still suffer from these memories as adults. My heart aches for these parents and children. I am blessed to say; I didn't encounter teasing as a child. Despite that, my advice to overcome this is that you continue pressing forward with a normal life. Attend birthday parties and playdates with your child, encourage them to join school clubs, and sports. Do all you can to let them know that their birthmark does not define who they are or can be.

"Ring the bells that still can ring. Forget your perfect offering. There is a crack, a crack in everything. That's how the light gets in."
Leonard Cohen

Living A Normal Life

The very first experience I recall living a normal life and finding my own voice was around 4th grade. I was elected "4th club president! I wasn't concerned about others not voting for me because of my birthmark. I was so thrilled because I knew others liked me. My mom was so excited for me! I also began playing basketball and reading in church. I was very active as a child. I wanted to be involved in everything. Little did I know that I was preparing myself for the attention that would come with being in the public eye. I began leading monthly meetings as well in front of my peers. I do recall an activity involving face painting. I felt a little apprehensive because I had no choice but to paint the left side of my face. I recall thoughts racing in my head, wondering if someone will make a joke about it but no one did. It's unfortunate that simple things such as face painting can cause so many fears and assumptions in a young person's mind.

_____

"Move out of your comfort zone. You can only grow if you are willing to feel awkward and uncomfortable when you try something new."
Brian Tracy

_____

The Moment I Realized, I Was Different!

I was a member of the youth church choir. Once a month our choir would sing at various churches. I loved singing. There were many of my friends from school in the children's choir as well. One Sunday, we sang at a Catholic church, and I recall we had on blue and white t-shirts that read "Cunningham C.M.E." I loved skorts. I had on a blue jean skort with knee length blue socks and doc martin shoes. We were all seated together center stage. After we sung our selection and were seated, I made eye contact with an elderly lady in the audience. She kept making a hand gesture indicating for me to remove my birthmark. I put my head down and pretended not to notice her. I barely raised my head again when I saw her doing the same thing. I put my head down again. At the end of the service, the pastor asked the congregation if anyone had any final remarks. Having a birthmark is like a constant feeling of being the spotlight. You just know when someone is about to ask you a question and you know if the statement will be polite or embarrassing. It's like second nature. At this moment, I felt in my soul that this question would pertain to my birthmark. Suddenly, the woman who had been gesturing to me stood up! My heart began to race!

She said, "Stand up young lady!" I kept my head down and pretended as if she wasn't talking to me hoping she would realize she was embarrassing me and have a seat. No such luck, she said it again. My cousin who was sitting right next to me stood up. The lady said, "Not you, the young lady beside you." I was always taught to respect my elders, so I just stood up.

She said, "Pastor, I've been making eye contact with this young lady to remove what's on her face, but I realized she can't." The pastor didn't say a thing. He immediately redirected his gaze and asked for any other remarks from the congregation. The lady sat down but continued to stare. I was so embarrassed. I felt alone, although my mother was in the audience. Thoughts started racing through my head. I felt as if now, my peers may treat me differently. My friends will feel sorry for me, and although everyone seemed to like me for me, they will start to stare and think only about my birthmark. No one will see me, for me. My eyes filled with water. I was so hurt. That was the first time I realized I was different!

My mother was equally as upset during our ride home. I remember her being furious, saying, "Why couldn't she wait until after church if she had a question about your birthmark?" I didn't say anything. I continued to hold back the tears, and I remember just staring out of the window. At that moment, I was building strength from within, and I didn't realize it. I was being strong for my mother. I felt she was embarrassed as well. Not because of my birthmark, but embarrassed for me. That was the first time my mom asked me if I wanted to remove it and how I really felt about it. I said no! I said no because I was scared of what I would have to go through during the surgery.

"This is the moment parents dread. The day their child is affected by stares or insensitive remarks. My mom could no longer fight my battles for me. My battles had begun."

Days went by, and I continued replaying this embarrassing moment in my head. I can paint a picture of this lady because I studied her for minutes before she spoke up because she made eye contact with me. I was hurting so deeply inside, but I continued to hide my pain. It's so ironic how I was being judged by adults and not my peers at school.

Imagine a child who battles being different within the community, school, and at home? There is no happy medium. I strongly encourage a loving household for your child. This moment could have been difficult to bear if my mother had not embraced my birthmark and or if she had constantly expressed her desire to remove it. I could have been a depressed child and possibly suffer from mental illness.

Emma Watson

Some time later I told my mom I wanted to remove my birthmark. That incident had affected me more than I thought. I was embarrassed. She asked me if I was sure and I said yes. We stopped to visit my grandmother before we left. God bless her soul, I will never forget her words. "Bae, please don't remove your birthmark." We drove to New Orleans, Louisiana and spoke to a plastic surgeon at Tulane Hospital. I was excited on the way there because I felt this was the end and I won't have to deal with another embarrassing moment. We parked in the garage and took the elevator to the hospital. I recall a man staring at me on the elevator. He gave me a weird look, and I could almost see the "what is that?" written on his forehead. Thinking about this moment now I wonder, why would an adult stare at a child with disgust? It's unbelievable how ignorant and rude some adults can be. He didn't have to ask any questions; his facial expressions said it all!

"I honestly feel that if you're not strong enough, people in the world can make you hate yourself. I believe that everyone would embrace their individuality more if people weren't so cruel."

The entire time the thought racing through my head was, "Only a few more stares and this will be all over." We met with the plastic surgeon, and he explained I would undergo a process called "tissue expansion." Being that my birthmark is on my right cheek, he would implant my skin directly underneath my birthmark, and extra skin would grow. However, it would take four months for enough skin to grow to replace my birthmark. Once the skin is fully grown, he would cut my birthmark out and place the new skin on top. I recalled frowning with disgust, "Like, are you serious? I'd walk around with extra skin hanging from my cheek?" He told me to think about it. He also said parents usually begin this process during the summer time, so children do not have to undergo the embarrassment at school. He took pictures of my birthmark and conducted a few tests to make sure it wasn't cancerous. My mom and I had time to consult, and I told her I was not walking around with extra growing skin for four months! She didn't like the idea as well, so we decided to head home.

On the way home, I broke down and cried. I told my mom I was so tired of people staring at me and making weird faces. I couldn't leave my hometown without someone questioning me. I didn't want to relive an embarrassing moment ever in life. My mom said, "Ferrin, you are beautiful! God made you in his image, and everyone won't understand. You are so pretty! There are children in wheelchairs, fighting cancer, leukemia, sickle cell, lupus, and you have a birthmark, that's it." I continued to cry. She asked me if I blamed her for having a birthmark on my face? I said no, and honestly, I didn't. I never felt it was my mother's fault.

When we arrived home, I locked myself in the bathroom, and I began studying my birthmark. I traced it with my finger. I rubbed it and smiled at myself. The mirror was my best friend. The mirror was my escape! My escape from people, wandering eyes, and unpredictable comments. In the mirror,

I'm the only one staring. I'm the only one with an opinion, and most importantly, I'm the only one with an opinion that matters.

I used to talk to myself so much as a child. I would say things such as, "Girl, let them look you are pretty!" "It's just a birthmark, relax." "Yes, God placed it here because he knew you could handle it, lady!"

"If I can see pain in your eyes, then share with me your tears. If I can see joy in your eyes, then share with me your smile."

Santosh Kalwar

The Cycle

A few weeks later, I began to feel refreshed again. I accepted the fact that I have a birthmark and finally went back to enjoying my childhood but, little did I know that this will be a lifelong progress. As a child, I don't recall seeing one person with a facial birthmark. Not one! Google was not a click away. I couldn't log on Instagram and search the "birthmark" hashtag or hop on Facebook and notice others who look like me. There also wasn't a Barbie doll or stuffed animal that looked the way I do.

I have to commend my mother for keeping me busy with extracurricular activities. My mind stayed at ease because I was constantly busy. I couldn't babysit my emotions. The incident from church eventually faded into the recesses of my mind. I had closure because I thought I'd never see the lady or attend that church again. However, I can vividly recall this incident as if it was yesterday.

I didn't know how many battles were ahead of me. I began paying more attention to people's reactions when they would stare. It was like a continuous cycle. I would overcome one encounter then face another one. I spoke to my mom about the stares, and she encouraged me to smile when I notice stares. That didn't always work because some people would look away quickly so I wouldn't notice them looking. But I always noticed.

-- -- -- -- -- -- -- -- -- -- -- -- -- -- -- --

"You stare at me because I'm
different, I stare because
you are all the same."
Unknown

-- -- -- -- -- -- -- -- -- -- -- -- -- -- -- --

Soap Suds

As time passed, I began experiencing more reactions, in which some where positive. I had a huge slumber party for my 10th birthday! I had 15 girls in attendance at my home. We had so much fun. We danced and sang all night long. Before bed, one of my friends asked to rub soap on my birthmark because she thinks it will be soft. I was shocked because others tagged along with us to the bathroom. It was so funny having my friends rub soap on my skin and say "Ooh, it's so soft, can we all rub it?" It made me feel good because it was a compliment and no one was freaked out about it. We were laughing and giggling. It's amazing that someone thought rubbing soap on my face was fun. Surprisingly, this took place in the same mirror I used as my escape! I had friends looking within my view as well. The mirror reflected positivity! I'm sure my childhood friend had no idea how much this meant to me or perhaps doesn't even remember but thank you, Timaria. My friends never asked about my birthmark. I'm sure they may have asked their parents in private, but when we were together, my birthmark didn't matter. We played in each other's hair, sang and danced the night away!

"The best and most beautiful things in this world cannot be seen or even heard, but it must be felt with the heart."
Helen Keller

Game Ready

Middle school is a big deal for children and their parents. There's more responsibility, older kids, new teachers, hormones, puberty, and the list goes on. It was during this time of my life I decided to try out for the cheerleading team. I seriously loved being in everything! I made the cheerleading team. During the games, it was normal to meet the cheerleaders from the opposing team during halftime. Most of the cheerleaders from the opposing team assumed my birthmark was face paint for the game. Most of the time I just went along with it because I didn't feel like explaining and I was okay with them thinking that. If someone would say, "Cool paint," my response would be "Game ready!" Sometimes I didn't feel like talking about my birthmark. Yes, my birthmark is on my face, and it's the first thing anyone notices, but it doesn't define the person I am. I enjoyed cheering at games, and I never felt stares from the crowd. As previously mentioned, so many people were familiar with seeing me around town. I also was elected as student council secretary and beta club president while in middle school. While leading these clubs, I didn't worry if my peers were listening to me or staring at my birthmark. I enjoyed leading.

I also had my first crush in middle school. Love notes were popular in middle school before everyone had cell phones. Well, I received a love note from an 8th grader. He said I was very pretty and asked if I would you go out with him. I responded and said yes. Not once did he mention my birthmark. We began walking to school together in the mornings. I recall asking him why he chose me. He said, "Because you caught my eye!" My confidence got a boost! I had a puppy love relationship that my mother knew absolutely nothing about. Eventually, she found out and my walks to school in the morning came to an end. I mention this because I want you to understand that I was a regular girl, well liked and popular. I became well known with the upperclassmen as well. This was the stage of my life when I began wearing eye shadow and lip gloss. I continued locking myself in the bathroom staring into the mirror, having my self-esteem boost conversations and tracing my birthmark with my finger and just smiling. Many times I would ask to be excused from class because I needed the restroom. But I didn't need the restroom; I just wanted to look at myself and trace the shape of my birthmark again. I had a small mirror in my purse as well, and I would gaze into it during class. I never realized how much others paid attention to me until I began hearing comments about me being conceited. Girls began to dislike me tremendously. How ironic right? My confidence began to intimidate others.

"Being one of a kind means we are automatically the best in the world at what we do."
Victor Williamson

When I hear stories about bullying in middle schools, it saddens me because some kids will never experience the joy of being accepted by others. When you are bullied or embarrassed about something, everything bothers you. You see a group of kids laughing and joking, and you may make eye contact with one person within that group and assume they are laughing at you. You miss events such as football games, basketball games, and school dances because you are ashamed. Or you might have trouble making friends because you feel they will see you as weird. I survived middle school because my head was held high. I involved myself in so many activities and didn't isolate myself from others. I'm sure if I wasn't as actively involved things would have been different. I strongly encourage you to do things you like. Do not let your birthmark stop you from excelling in anything. Everyone has something they enjoy doing. Don't keep yourself in a box; try new things as well!

If you are being teased while trying to live a normal life as possible, begin standing up for yourself. The first time someone teases you, it will be extremely hard, but you will eventually reach a breaking point. It's okay to practice walking with your head high and practicing rebuttals. Journaling also helps. Keep track of your experiences and emotions; it's something ycu can look back to in future and be proud of the things you have overcome.

Sometimes I wonder what my perspective would be if I didn't have a birthmark. How would I react if I saw one for the first time? Ask yourself, how do you react when you see something different? Do you squint your eyes? Do you verbally inquire to educate yourself? Speaking for myself, I don't stare at anything I notice as different on someone because I know how it feels to be in their shoes. I deliberately respect cthers in this regard. Some people have a hard time doing this. I've caught so many people staring at me, and the reactions are sometimes hilarious. I would rather someone respectfully ask about my birthmark than stare brazenly. Of course, some people will stare no matter what. I advise you to take these stares head on. For example, if you are in a grocery store and someone is staring at you in the aisle, don't run to the next aisle, there may be five more people on the next aisle. Is it annoying? Absolutely! But maybe they never saw a walking god or goddess before!

_ . _ . _ . _ . _ . _ . _ . _ . _ . _ . _ . _ . _ . _ . _ . _ . _ . _ . _ . _ -

"Never be bullied into silence. Never allow yourself to be made a victim. Accept no one's definition of your life; define yourself."
Harvey Fierstein

_ . _ . _ . _ . _ . _ . _ . _ . _ . _ . _ . _ . _ . _ . _ . _ . _ . _ . _ . _ -

The Eye Of The Tiger

I decided in the 8th grade to play basketball for the community. My stepdad was a great player and taught me a few moves. Unfortunately, I could only shoot 3 point shots. I wasn't good, so basically that's all I was known for. I began playing a few games, and high school guys within the community would attend. Well, a teammate informed me that one of the guys were calling me "Tiger stripe." When she told me, I wondered if she was telling me this to bring my spirits down or just really informing me. It bothered me, and I wasn't sure who exactly had said those words until he made himself known. One day I walked past the bleachers to warm up, and I heard him say "Tiger stripe." I pretended not to hear him. He didn't let up either. He would say it so much it discouraged me from playing basketball. Every game I would pray he wasn't there so I wouldn't have to hear those words. Well, I have had a lot of time to reflect on those words, so I have a thing or two to say about a tiger and its stripes.

Tigers move with confident, regal strides. They are bold and fierce in all they do.

I also reflect upon the eye of the tiger. The tiger makes eye contact seconds before an attack. Have you ever been somewhere and raised your head only to lock eyes with someone staring at you? People fear the eye of the tiger because they do not know what's coming. Think of yourself as a Tiger, will you walk away with a confident stride or will you shy away and feel sorry for yourself? Remember, Tigers are not shy! Sometimes, people don't realize to what they are comparing you. The symbolic meaning can be sufficient fact about how strong you are!

There will be days when you won't feel like defending your birthmark or explaining to everyone what it is. Years ago, I noticed that on my weary days I began doing repetitive things such as shopping at stores where I was well known and pumping gas at the same station. I began to be afraid of change. I'd prefer the company of the same people with whom I had grown comfortable. Little did I know that I had subjected myself to living in a 'box.' I was scared of words and afraid to hear something negative because I was not completely comfortable in my skin. Don't live like that. Be free. Expand your world by trying new things and meeting new people.

- -

"Silly words cause trills because they're ludicrous and funny. Happy words paint endless smiles and swallow troubles whole. Thoughtful words are thus because they make the day feel sunny. But hurtful words are such that pierce the heart and weigh the soul."

Richelle E. Goodrich

- -

8th grade was also the year I became an older sister! My little Teryn was the best baby sister ever.

She was such a happy baby! I don't recall her asking about my birthmark. I think she was used to seeing me with it. I had a conversation with her when she was younger and told her what it was. She just smiled. The older she became, the more I saw myself in her eyes. Teryn is now a teenager. She takes pictures with me, compliments me daily and is proud to be my sister. I've met several of her friends and according to her everyone says, "Your sister is so pretty with that birthmark thing." She invites me to school programs, dance recitals, etc.

It's important for parents to sit and talk to siblings to find out their feelings as well. Educate them on birthmarks and how it's okay to love their sibling and be mindful of their feelings.

"If you are faced with a mountain, you have several options. You can climb it and cross to the other side. You can go around it. You can dig under it. You can fly over it. You can ignore it and pretend its not there. You can turn around and go back the way you came. Or you can stay on the mountain and make it your home."

Vera Nazarian

Joy Ride

My high school years were some of the best years of my life. I was a little nervous Freshman year because I didn't know how some would react to my birthmark. I eventually met the guy who would call me "tiger stripe." Apparently, he had shortened it to "Tiger" at the time. I began to find it amusing because he would say it with so much base in his voice. It didn't bother me anymore. One day, we talked, and I told him my name was Ferrin. He said, "I like Tiger better." I found myself laughing again. I wonder how I would've reacted to meeting him if I hadn't built my confidence in myself.

I also began learning more about true authentic friendships at this age. It's important to have positive people around you. If you are attending a new school and don't know anyone, engage in conversation. Listen for who needs to borrow a pen. Be kind. It's okay if you have a few lone days but pay attention to the people around you. Someone else might be feeling the same way.

It is the tradition in senior year to vote for class favorite, most likely to succeed, best athlete, most attractive female/male, favorite couples, and most reliable. Well, I, along with another female student, was selected as most attractive! This was also confirmation that my student body saw me for me! During graduation, our class also made funny jokes and I'll never forget the joke where someone stated, "10 years from now Ferrin Francis will still be looking in a mirror saying "Do I look okay? Is my hair in place?" I really took pride in the way I looked. I would become so upset if I had a pimple on my face! That's because I accepted my birthmark as a part of me but not pimples on my face!

Also, plenty of guys asked me out, and I always had a date to every school function. I was asked to prom as a freshman, but my mom didn't allow it. However, I attended junior and senior prom. I was also on the homecoming court. High school was amazing!

However, it is important to know that it's okay if no one asks you to any of these events! I encourage you to attend anyway. You may attend and realize that you're not missing a thing! At least you have the experience and can decide if you enjoy these types of events.

"Be different. Be original. Nobody will remember a specific flower in a garden filled with thousands of the same yellow flower, but they will remember the one that managed to change its color to purple"
Suzy Kaseem

Hidden Birthmarks

Let's talk about invisible birthmarks. Many people hide their insecurities, suffer mentally from problems at home or have broken hearts and pretend to be happy. I refer to them as having a hidden birthmark. These are unseen marks or scars on their hearts. Everyone battles with something. Sometimes others may choose to target you for your birthmark because it takes the attention off what they are hiding. By unveiling my birthmark, I am declaring my boldness! People are so afraid of what others think and say, so of course your smile and birthmark will be intimidating to someone who does not love themselves. People hide behind fancy cars, clothes, and material things. View your birthmark as your strength and encouragement to others whose scars are hidden.

---·--

"You are a rainbow that rarely appears, but when you do, your presence is felt and noticed."
Ferrin Roy

---·--

Birthmark Rebirth

I attended college at Southern University in Baton Rouge, Louisiana. Bye, bye small town, hello to the city! I was excited to attend college but little did I know that my birthmark was going to be reborn in this city. All the growth stages and obstacles I had conquered seemed in vain during this time in my life. This period was when I really felt what others may have experienced attending a new school. I survived elementary, middle, and high school but now I faced adulthood. This was the hardest phase of my life during the age of 18-25. There were times I would forget I had a birthmark on my face until I noticed someone staring in class, the library, or at the bookstore. I couldn't determine if I was being admired or judged. I'd always been friendly so I would engage in normal conversation but would feel their eyes focusing on my birthmark and not on what I was saying. As an adult, I didn't feel the need to make my birthmark the topic of discussion. I would answer if someone asked, but I didn't feel the need to explain myself. The stares were like daggers, and I felt them over and over again. Every time I walked to class or passed by a group of people, it was a new set of daggers. The stares were so constant that I began questioning myself about being an educator. I wondered if my students would focus on my birthmark and not concentrate on learning.

College consisted of several group projects. I became friends with a guy from a group project who informed me about twin girls who recently graduated, both had facial birthmarks. He tried to find them in a yearbook but he couldn't. He was the first guy to ask me on a date in college. He was a very nice guy, but I only wanted friendship with him. Just because I had a birthmark didn't mean I had to date anyone who was interested.

I encourage you not to feel sorry for yourself or feel you have to date whoever asks you because maybe you think no one else will be interested. Everyone has likes and dislikes. Although people still stared at me, I was approached by several guys. I never felt the need to give anyone a chance who was interested in me or complimented my birthmark. I never felt the need to just "go along" with anyone who showed me attention.

As college progressed, I began meeting some wonderful people. I decided to pursue Family & Consumer Science with a concentration in Child Development. This program also required student observation and minimal student teaching. I recall walking down the hallway at an elementary school and a cute little girl asked me to follow her. She led me to a little girl with a birthmark. I was so happy to see her. I watched her through the window and smiled envisioning myself at this age. I didn't want to embarrass her because I was unsure of what her perception of her birthmark was at that young age. I waited until recess and approached her. I told her she was special just like me. She smiled and continued running around with her friends. That was the day I knew I wanted to counsel and motivate others. I loved seeing her face brighten up with delight. It made my day to allow her to see someone who looks like her.

---·-·--·-·--·-·--·-·--·-·--·-·--·-·--·-·--·-·--·

"There is no exercise better for the
heart than reaching down and
lifting people up."
John Holmes

---·-·--·-·--·-·--·-·--·-·--·-·--·-·--·-·--·-·--·

Opinions

I believe I am a very friendly person. I respect others, and I'm very understanding. I've spoken with so many people from across the world on Instagram and Facebook who are living with birthmarks. Our birthmark community is actively growing. We empower each other to live life unashamed and continue being an example for others. I love when I receive messages from teens who are struggling with acceptance. I try my best to encourage them to love themselves no matter what others say. One teen stated, witnessing my confidence inspires her to be happy! It touched my heart because that's exactly the message I want to portray. I also spoke to a parent who said her son hadn't smiled in months until he saw me smiling with my birthmark. I often post pictures of others with birthmarks on my social media page to boost their confidence and self-esteem. We are learning the importance of valuing our opinion and not others. I've always loved my birthmark, but there were times I'd allow people and their opinions to make me feel different. I will never understand why people feel the need to bring others down; besides misery. I also don't understand why others are so concerned about something that is not a part of them. If you see someone who is different and they are smiling, don't dampen their smile because of your inquisitiveness.

"They wore their strange beauty like war paint."
Holly Black

Think about the things people do to themselves to be different or stand out. Some women dye their hair bright colors, some men and women tattoo their faces, and some may pierce their skin. Clothing trends are changing as well. No one gives an opinion about these things because they're common and accepted, but with birthmarks or scars, people are so judgmental. We need to do better as a society.

While shopping in the mall one day, a young man stopped me and asked if my birthmark was a tattoo. When I told him it was my birthmark, he said, "You are so beautiful, and you really stand out. People try so hard to be different, and you are just being you and its looks great on you."

"Having a low opinion of yourself is not modesty. It's self-destruction. Holding your uniqueness in high regard is not egotism. It's a necessary precondition to happiness and success."

Bobbe Sommer

Magic Tricks

A few years passed by and in 2009 I became a mother! It was such an indescribable feeling. It was love at first sight! During this time, I also began undergoing relationship challenges that made me feel the weight of the world was on my shoulders. I lost myself and forgot who I was as an individual. I began accepting things that I shouldn't. I forgot my self-worth, and my confidence dropped drastically. While shopping one day, a man approached me saying "Birthmarks are evil." I walked away from him because I didn't feel like defending my birthmark, again! He began following me around the store. He would walk away then come back again. I decided to check out of the store because I was upset and was starting to get scared as well. He approached the counter and said, "My ex-wife and daughter have birthmarks on their faces, and I said a prayer, and it went away." I told him I was uninterested in his magic tricks. "You are mean just like my ex-wife and daughter," he said. "The birthmark is making you mean just like them." He began following me to my car and pulling on my arm. I dropped all my belongings and started to call the cops; then he ran away! People began coming out of the store and asking if I was okay. I said yes, but I was in pain.

I called my mother crying, and I told her I couldn't take it anymore. I told her I was sick of defending my birthmark and sick of people staring at me. My mother told me to pray about it and not to make sudden decisions. I was so furious I couldn't pray. I didn't want to pray. I just wanted to be left alone. I didn't run to my mirror like I did as a little girl and admire myself anymore. I couldn't sleep at night because I was replaying this incident. I started to dislike people and how disrespectful and rude they were. There were times I was tempted to say things like, *you don't have a birthmark, and I still don't find your look appealing!* to some people who would approach me and say mean things. But what's the use of being mean to them just because they were to me? People don't realize others with birthmarks or scars, etc. has opinions as well. But I'm very respectful of others, and I never allowed myself to decrease others self-esteem because they are trying to decrease mine. Instead, I began researching others with birthmarks in search of their experiences as well. I discovered the birthmark foundation online. I connected with a few parents over email who would send encouragement daily. I sent out an email about the encounter I had, and the responses I received were so helpful. Everyone said how sorry they were that I went through this. Others were also in agreement about society and how rude people are. It felt good to speak to others who could relate. People use the term "I understand" too loosely. If you don't have a birthmark, you don't understand.

I scheduled an appointment with a plastic surgeon. He decided to use my birthmark as a case study. The study revealed the exact procedure I was informed about many years ago, the tissue expansion. I was still upset, and I didn't know what to do. I was angry all the time. I truly didn't want to remove my birthmark, but I felt forced to.

"It is our wounds that create in us a desire to reach for miracles. The fulfillment of such miracles depends on whether we let our wounds pull us down or lift us up towards our dreams."

Jocelyn Soriano

Falling On My Knees

I finally took my mother's advice. I fell to my knees, and I prayed. I asked God what is my purpose in life and why He was taking me through so much. Why did He choose me to have a birthmark? Why do I survive one stage of my life only to start the cycle over again? I begged God to please reveal to me what He wanted me to do.

I pray every night on my knees. I've always asked God to reveal my purpose to me, but I never prayed to understand why I have a birthmark. This same night God spoke to me through a dream. He revealed to me the need to write a book and explain my experiences to help others. My book was clear as day in my dream. The chapters are titled based on experiences.

"For I know the plans I have for you,"
declares the Lord, "plans to prosper
you and not to harm you, plans to
give you hope and a future."
Jeremiah 29:11

I've had so many dreams that I couldn't fully remember when I woke up. But not this dream. I remember it vividly. I began writing my book the next morning. I called my mom with so much excitement. The power of prayer! I began thinking about the times I would search the web and notice others finding their unique niche. So many women were opening online boutiques, monogramming clothes, making jewelry, etc. I would try these things as well because I felt like I could do it too. I recognized others' special gifts and talents, and I wanted to make them my own. This is a common mistake so many people make. Everyone has a unique and special gift. It cannot be duplicated! You may notice what others are doing and begin to mimic them, but it won't last. God allowed me to imitate others and fail with the several small businesses I attempted to start. Once I surrendered and grew tired of these small businesses failing, my gift and purpose was revealed to me. The entire time I was searching to learn my purpose in life, it was right in front of me, on my face! The mirror I would look into as a little girl, the reflection of me, within my view, was my gift!

After this turning point in my life, I vowed never to allow anyone take me down such a dark path. It is a true statement "God will use your enemies as a footstool." I gained my complete confidence back, I'm constantly in the mirror and loving the skin I'm in. I am comfortable in my skin. I feel so good about myself! My birthmark is now my beauty mark!

I debated talking about my spiritual journey because there are people who blame God for their pain. There are also people who do not believe. However, God is what got me through, not a psychiatrist, or a plastic surgeon. Plastic surgery may have stopped a few stares but what would it have done for me internally? I would have been another insecure person living for the approval of others and trying to change everything about myself. What would have been next? My hair, my nose, or my lips?

Through their words, people have the power to make you feel useless if you let them. I used to be a person who wanted everyone to like me. I hated when people said horrible things about me. I hated being misunderstood. I went through a few relationships and friendships with people who took my kindness as weakness or frankly, didn't care about me. I've also dealt with women who didn't know themselves and who made my birthmark the topic of conversation as if that was enough to bring me down. Once you know who you are, no one can take that from you.

Ever since my deliverance, I don't pay attention if people are staring. I've evolved into such a confident woman. I live my life, and I don't care who is watching. I am free from people!

I've been featured in several articles discussing my confidence. It's unbelievable how many people approach me with compliments. When you are ashamed of something, it shows. When you are confident people have no choice but to accept you for who you are. If I were to hear something negative about my birthmark today, I wouldn't care! I love myself!

S. J. R.

Once I evolved as a woman, I met the most amazing man that God kept in store for me. If I had met my husband a year month, or day sooner, I wouldn't have been ready. Before you can love someone unconditionally, you have to love yourself first. You also have to know what you want out of life. I don't mean you have to have it all together, but it's just important you know who you are as an individual. I am in love with the man God chose for me, Shavayne J. Roy! Sometimes I find myself just staring at him in disbelief. I truly had no idea what was in store for me. When I informed him about my book, he was completely supportive. He makes me feel secure with him. I feel safe, supported, protected, and unconditionally loved. The little things he does such as kissing and rubbing my birthmark makes me smile. I interviewed my husband to help my readers who may be wondering if love is in store for them. I wanted you all to have some personal insight about how he feels as well. If you are dating someone and you feel they do not love you for you, don't force it. I believe in moving on. I believe in passionate, extraordinary LOVE!

FR: What were your initial thoughts when you first noticed me?

SJR: The first time I laid eyes on you, my initial thought was that I've never seen anyone with a birthmark on their face. I was intrigued by you, and I said to myself, "I have to get to know her. I was amazed by your beauty. You weren't ashamed of it, and I admired that about you. You have so much confidence, and I'll always adore this about you.

FR: How do you feel when someone asks you about my birthmark?

SJR: Honestly, I get excited to speak about your birthmark. I find myself in deep conversation as if your birthmark was on my face.

FR: How would you react if someone said something negative about it?

SJR: As your husband, I would defend you because your birthmark is a part of you and you are a part of me.

FR: How would you feel if our children had birthmarks?

SJR: If our kids have birthmarks, I would feel the same way and love them just as I love you with yours.

FR: How do you feel about people staring at me?

SJR: I figure they never laid eyes on someone so beautiful. They are shocked by how distinguished you are.

"The best love is the kind that awakens the soul and makes us reach for more, that plants fire in our hearts and brings peace to our minds. And that's what you've given me. That's what I'd hope to give you forever."

Nicholas Sparks

My Children,
My Angels

I have two beautiful little girls. Hailyn is seven and Aavyn is four. Neither of them has facial birthmarks. Birthmarks are not hereditary. During both pregnancies, I was asked several times how I would feel if my girls had birthmarks. My response to everyone was "my hope is for a healthy baby." During a prenatal visit, I met a woman with a birthmark directly on her forehead. It was also a nevus as well. She told me that if her child had a birthmark, she'd remove it because she feels society will destroy her child. I felt differently, but I respected her opinion. I completely understood her reason for feeling so strongly about it. My purpose is to show people who are living with birthmarks and scars a different perspective; to encourage them to be happy regardless of what society feels about their appearance.

Hailyn is the spitting image of me. The second she learned how to talk, I taught her about my birthmark. She also can recognize birthmarks on others as well. When I asked her what she thinks about it, she said, "Mama, I look just like you, will I get one when I grow up?" She always says I'm pretty. She doesn't ask any questions. I am her mother; I strive to be a great example for her!

Aavyn is funny! Aavyn rubs my birthmark every day. I mean every single day! She says it's soft and fun. She also asked why she doesn't have one. She likes to pretend that she has one and asks me to rub her face. She loves to rub it when we're cuddling and watching movies.

I've explained to both of my daughters that it's ok to be different and to be friends with children who do not look like them. I've worked as an autism therapist before. Hailyn job shadowed a few times. I loved watching her interact with autistic children. She was so helpful and enjoyed being around them. I want my children to be exposed to differences and not become judgmental. We also discuss children who are in wheelchairs and children who are battling diseases. They are taught not to stare. I encourage them to smile and be kind to everyone.

"Hailyn & Aavyn, do not allow anyone to change your perception of yourself. You two are beautiful girls inside and out. Mommy will continue setting an example for you both and your future siblings."

The Cycle Is Broken!

One of the happiest moments in your life will be when you find the courage to let go of what you cannot change. I hope this book, my testimony, and my experiences, inspires you to be happy and continue living your life unashamed. When you accept your birthmark, others will also. Once I accepted my birthmark as an asset, stares stopped bothering me. I remind myself that they are witnessing a walking goddess! Remember, you are a tiger with a confident stride and a rainbow that appears from time to time. People do not see faces that resemble yours often, but when they do, it's a face they will never forget and a heart everyone will fall in love with!

---.---.---.---.---.---.---.---.---.---.---.---.---.---.

"Broken Crayons still color."
Unknown

---.---.---.---.---.---.---.---.---.---.---.---.---.---.

My Mirror

While gazing into my mirror, I see a strong, courageous, confident and beautiful woman. I am fearless, bold, and unique. I've overcome the challenges which were meant to destroy me. I know my purpose, and I am living it.

I love myself, and I am loved. I am loved by my Savior Jesus Christ and my amazing husband. They are a part of my mirror. God made me in His perfect image and blessed me with someone who envisions what we see.

I am free! I am free from people and the shattered pieces of my mirror they tried to make me look into.

My mirror is clear, shatterproof, and in one piece.

THIS IS THE MARK I KEPT!

"Quotes to Inspire"

"Wear your birthmark with confidence." - **Ferrin Roy**

"Don't worry about hurting my feelings because I guarantee you not one bit of my self-esteem is tied up in your acceptance." - **Dr. Phil**

"If I can give you one gift, I would give you the ability to see yourself as I see you, so you can truly see how special you are." - **Unknown**

"High self-esteem does not happen overnight, you have to work at it, and that is completely okay."- **Unknown**

"No one can make you feel inferior without your consent." - **Eleanor Roosevelt**

"Wanting to be someone else is a waste of the person you are." - **Unknown**

"Make sure your worst enemy is not living between your two ears." - **Unknown**

"When you're different, sometimes you don't see the millions of people who accept you for what you are. All you notice is the person who doesn't. - **Jodi Picoult**

"There is no magic cure, no making it all go away forever. There are steps upward; an easier day, an unexpected laugh, a mirror that doesn't matter anymore." - **Laurie Halse Anderson**

Stay Connected

To continue following my journey, please subscribe to my website www.ferrinroy.com. Here you will find many articles, photos displaying confidence and future endeavors. I can also be found on Instagram: @Ferrin_Roy and Facebook: Ferrin Roy

Made in the USA
San Bernardino, CA
04 November 2017